The addendum to perfection

By Michael D. Brown

The addendum to perfection

The addendum to perfection

For my wife Stephanie, the woman I have secretly loved in romance novels

The addendum to perfection

Grateful acknowledge is made to the editors
of the following Journals, Magazines and Reviews
Where many of these poems first appeared:
Voices, The Geronimo Review, Three Cups, Awareness,
The Scroll, Ascent, Ink Pot, Literary Potpourri, and
Timbooktu.

The addendum to perfection

1) R.s.v.p
2) Slowly without breaking records for time
3) Enough
4) 911
5) What to do in a storm
6) Epistemology
7) Technique
8) H2o
9) I'd like to be the man
10) Life
11) Better this love
12) Sequel to youth
13) Punctual
14) For worst
15) Iris
16) Winter secrets #5
17) Syracuse
18) Summer
19) Insightful
20) Losing you
21) Keepsake
22) Feline
23) Bathsheba
24) Foreplay
25) Arousal
26) Making Love
27) Forever on its own
28) Volition
29) My question
30) Happy Birthday
31) Only this joy
32) Drawn
33) War
34) When spring returns
35) Cleaning
36) Compliant
37) Cooking
38) Ravages of war
39) Ecosystem
40) Rush hour
41) 24/7
42) For love
43) Sugar

The addendum to perfection

44) Recollection
45) My Beloved Valentine
46) Passions
47) Something touched me
48) Adultery
49) Biblical love
50) After conversation
51) Jewelry
52) Why
53) Drought
54) October
55) X
56) Sighting
57) Two goals
58) Such captions
59) In the laundry room
60) Skinny dipping
61) Hiding in tall grass
62) Perfection
63) The addendum to perfection
64) Amen

The addendum to perfection

R. s .v .p

Out of the certainty
That encroaches upon light

Given freely by stars-
A sort of stellar grace:

Waiting gently for recipients to open
The envelope, to read their names written

Embossed a heavenly body
With a title better than moon, in a book of life

With rings of rainbow, with a place reserved
For you and I.

The addendum to perfection

Slowly, without breaking records for time

I am determined to love you, slowly without breaking records for time.

The voice in my diaphragm speaks of sonnets, wafer thin, romantic,
like the rudder that steers the moon.

Together floating- a hollow lily pad- we rock back and forth with the motion of sailors adrift at sea.

We have become one breath for hours now. I move gently in sleep whenever your body moves, its pure science.

Morning does not pry things apart that can never become separate entities ever again.
We are compressed files in a data base.

We are lines drawn together that form our first and last name.
We are careful adjusting sunlight in each others eyes.

There is no more loneliness in our hearts.
Your fingers sketch open lines in my hands in cursive loops.

The secret between us is naked, ever reverberating.
Air breaths for itself each time I kiss you and you are the only thing that matters.

Why does this much happiness bring such strong tears?
The delicate weight of your body pins me on my back to surf the low tide.
My hands want to be in more places to draw you closer to the ecstasy, every time the tide
Returns in such a rush to shore. I have always been the sea, never pulling away from you,

Leaving starfish on the beach like an evening sky; wrapping myself around you to remain beautiful; to become handsome in your eyes. I am determined to love you slowly, without breaking records for time.

The addendum to perfection

Enough

She loved truly just once

And for so long,

And then, never again.

For to repeat is to take away,

Or so she felt and desired

Not to feel again; for the first

Was right and so right, it

Should also be the last,

An Alpha and Omega, and

The memory must be intact, untarnished,

And for someone new, to try,

would only mean

endless comparison

And certain defeat, and

When one has, what she had,

Then you never really lose it,

And it truly is, for a lifetime,

Enough!

911

For the victims and their families

The screams are not silent
In the terror of memories past.

But it is never only the past.
There are days that take on life in its own infamy.

Reports come to make news undesirable forever.
Death separates itself from life

As if they never were related, as a beginning, as an end.
Making sense of it all escapes every explanation

That the heart excepts as rational.
Every new day, in the wake of this day, laments in hope.

The addendum to perfection

What to do in a storm

I recommend facing south
When wind comes down

from the North both your hands
Sounding like chimes stretched

Out like a weather vane.
But what better way

To make love
Than in the rain? In a downpour

That won't allow anyone to see,
With their mouths opened wide

For sheer effect, for the shock
Of catching the umbrella opened,

Fully like a pleated skirt, over extended
The way trees lean

At the behest of strong wind.
I recommend facing south.

The addendum to perfection

Epistemology

Who can say how long
We have loved with our mouths closed,

Just plants waiting for rain, waiting for drops
To drench all the dry places, to unwring the drought

From its twisted knot, from its coil made of sand?
Who can tell from the puddle of our muddy lives,

From the children making dirt pies
Who can tell?

The addendum to perfection

Technique

I measure the combination of words

When I write poetry

By infinity.

I think to count words for every star

In every galaxy:

For every grain of sand

That wants to be numbered

Considered present and accounted for:

For every number that doubles as a word

And every word that wants to be a number:

For every letter that remains alphabetized

Until its called a word,

I measure the combination of words when I write poetry

By infinity.

The addendum to perfection

H2o

Compliment
The ocean

With a tide.
Love the mile

Into shore.
Sand will always wait

For the human touch.
The sun loves the beach

For all the hard bodies
That gravitate to tanned skin.

Water stays somewhere near the sea
Even if it has to evaporate.

I taste you salty on my tongue.
With my eyes closed
I can imagine
Almost anything.

The addendum to perfection

I'd like to be the man

Whose ring
Wears your finger

With marital pride.
Never removing

Or being removed
Vowing in the presence

Of witnesses
Of god

Virtues until
The parting of death

Which can only part
In one small sense

What took a lifetime to unite
Into a oneness

That needs two
To make the math work
To make the rhythm flow

Enough to be a verse.
I'd like to be that man

The addendum to perfection

Life

Yesterday came
Without the promise

Of today. I never look back
When I'm living so close

To tomorrow.
Looking is relative anyway

When things are gone
And here and coming.

The addendum to perfection

Better this love

Than anything past
That could only crouch

But not climb stars
With five points to hold

Like fingers pointing
Or reaching out for me

To grasp and never let go
Of dreams that we live

Each day together
For the magic of time

That slows and even holds still
Long enough for lips

To press the wrinkles
Out of loneliness

When they absorb
Tears and cause

Smiles to breakout
Of their straight face

And our posture
Is pure repose.

The addendum to perfection

The sequel to youth

What have I to do
With the distance between here

And oblivion?
I close gaps in space

every time I reinvent intimacies,
every time I allow myself the privilege

Of playfulness.
Children recognize adults

Who use to be one of them.
Now and then they bridge from here to there.

From where we are
From where we ought to be.

The addendum to perfection

Punctual

Wondered about love showing up late
When I would be older than anyone's memory

And the day would be so modern I could not
Go and find my way around in it.

Questioned if directions would help bring it
To my doorstep sooner.

I would even leave a key in the mailbox with a note
For a woman with a name like, Stephanie.

Thought weather could be a deterrent
But the sun never impeached the snow

When I was having fun.
Now its up to love to be on time.

The addendum to perfection

For worst

When I learned the ameba
 Loves only itself
 And always alone
  I embraced divorce.

The addendum to perfection

Iris

Arrive
On your birthday

Out of season
With an affinity

For the way water
Beads on your lips,
Lips that flower
In any good soil-

That plant wet kisses
In every sculpted curve on my face.

The addendum to perfection

Winter secrets #5

Winter sets apart trees naked
Behind the x-ray screen

White bones stark for limbs.
Trunks pulled up for warmth.

Bark clad like armor,
Like an ornament,

Remarkable for a temple.
Remarkable for a tree.

The addendum to perfection

Syracuse

Winter rents this space
Even during the off season.

Find the sun shining under
The curved eye of your microscope,

Above the report of overcast skies.
Around somewhere other than here.

Near us but not with us, at least not
For long or long enough to use

Phrases like, "summer vacation,"
Or "lets go running in the park."

No! this is Syracuse, N.Y.
And we will have none of that.

The addendum to perfection

Summer

Bask up the sun
When it rays on your skin

Like a lover loves to touch
And the heat from that caress tans

The milk in your skin brown
And the glow of that red undertone

Makes me hot and my blood rises
To the occasion
Of your summons
To love.

The addendum to perfection

Insightful

How many are insightful enough
To taste ions heavy in the air predicting a storm?

More than rain clean against my window
Swallowing nitrogen in a plant, waiting to breathe

As I breathe in your presence for the moment
That I move close and holding you is new and near perfection.

If only just this one moment in my forever
That has to pause before you, knees bent, flowers opening in a shift,

How many?

The addendum to perfection

Losing you

Defeats the purpose
Of my contagious smile.

The indomitable Spirit
That sends and moves

Within the wind
In my every breath

Remains still.
Dying is easy in your absence

And practice makes me perfect.
The setting of the sun

Is 35mm
Of photographic color.

I picture your departure
The same

The addendum to perfection

Keepsake

Roses become parchment like paper
With their white layers of silk skin.

No wrinkle ever numbers their age.
Every detail has its own perfection

Engraved deep for a signature.
The bulb still cups in hope of water

Like your lips wet with the dew
Of our every contact.

Sheer on the print of your lacey contour
Breathing as it hugs, holding until I bring them new

For a memory that dozens in a shift
On your lap like a rose.

The addendum to perfection

Feline

Not only of mice and men
But of women and cats.

Some Siamese with eyes
Twice Egyptian even Cleopatra.

Everything feline curls
In a ball when it purrs

On my lap like a lover
Lapping milk in short silent strokes.

The lateral movement of the tail
Is dual hypnotic seduction.

Only my eyes follow
All the way South to the Nile.

The addendum to perfection

Bathsheba

My woman sunbathes.
Water encircles her perfect form

With ripples in the lake.
Her reflection is a refracted original.

The artist in me grids
Every section of her frame,

Proportionate by design.
Her body clothed in light

And stroked by air.
Bathsheba bathed in the eyes of David.

It is good to be the king!

The addendum to perfection

Foreplay

The river flows
Like the current that runs in me.

Water compares its own necessity
To move with my need to advance

To where ever you are.
I gaze for hours into your eyes

Never fearing the strength of the sun.
I have never removed any clothing

And loving you has never been this easy.

The addendum to perfection

Arousal

I was safe without this desire
Not seeking or being sought

Not touching or being touched.
Dormant in the cave of hibernation.

But there came this chemistry
In the curve of a woman

So completely feminine.
Her voice so soft with texture

She only had to speak.

The addendum to perfection

Making love

I see us in front of the fireplace, smoldering
Licking flames that dance, that passionate dance,

Over each log that rolls without moving, like I move
And you roll when we are logs together and on fire.

Stacked for the beauty of heat and the warmth
Of the hearth in both our hearts

that no winter can dowse
With its own artic glory.

The addendum to perfection

Forever on its own

I do not know why I thought
There would be an ending

before our love reached forever
On its own.

Perhaps the common
Interruptions like divorce

Or its twin sister death.
Maybe it was the uncertainty

Of the future that caused me to flinch
Without the consideration of faith.

I think about commitments
That I cannot keep long enough to question

What motivates me to make them.
It must be the desire that wants things to last.

The feeling that something good can survive
Any diminishing return-
The unlimited resource I find in your love.
I do not know why I thought

There would be and ending
Before our love reached

forever on its own.

The addendum to perfection

Volition

More feminine than the rising sun
The moon curves

Dressed in a single white polka dot
Like the spot you left on my heart

With your bottle of whiteout, your intention
To fill the void with commitments

Only a signature can make.
I license you to freedom of choice.

The addendum to perfection

My question

When you say the words,
"I love you"

Are you words double blind?
Randomized, placebo controlled?

Or am I suppose to trust?
To listen with my middle inner ear?

To see with two myopic eyes

the truth?

The addendum to perfection

Happy Birthday

Forgive three hundred, sixty four days
For they can never be today.

Fifty-one weeks for they are not this week.
-eleven months that can only blowout

The candles on someone else's cake.
Forgive every smile that arrives disarmed,

A belated wish, for this day, different
From all other days.

Forgive these simple words for wishing
They were more, much more

Than just mere words on this day
Different from every other day.

The addendum to perfection

Only this joy

Your name brings me fortune every time it slants cursive
In Arabic and stands upright English on my tongue.

Whispers between us remain in the air long, long enough
To echo then resound, in our ears, ears that sprout leaves

The same color Jade I find in your soul.
I enter the inner court where no one has ever been allowed.

You wrap yourself around me and your love on my skin is my air,
My resuscitation.

I resign myself to know only this joy.

The addendum to perfection

Drawn together

How can we survive years
Without the necessity of love?

Shouldn't we be drawn together
Like magnets with their negative and positive polarity?

Like the sun following closely
Behind the rain for as much contact

As dew is allowed to sparkle?
Like clouds gather in clusters

Only to disperse when the wind
Appears puckered up, circling

To reveal both halves of a full moon
Joined together?

Shouldn't we also
With my masculine ying,

And your feminine yang
Be drawn together.

The addendum to perfection

War

Bombs fall from B52's
Like dead bodies into open graves.

Their weight is deafening in the air.
The sound of life exploding is muffled

By the screams of children cradled
Behind their mothers veil.

Nothing in the black sky
Is ever calm again.

The addendum to perfection

When spring returns

On days like this
When rain redefines everything that use to be dry

My eyes remember you with tears.
The basement floods whenever drains backup this much

And I recall the former things as if they were still present
With me today.

Trees appreciate rain for the darker shade of green
They appear to have.

Your Olive tone remains a fixture in my mind.
You look Mediterranean on certain days with a mixture of sun.

I have yet to adjust to your moving south for the winter
Since the spring won't return this year.

The addendum to perfection

Cleaning the yard

Today I found this old penny in the yard.
Its brown enough to be the ground camouflaged

Underneath wet leaves.
The spring returns no matter

How many of them we spend without discretion.
I want to keep a lid on the one that preserves

The long harsh winters.
Summers would sell for whatever the market will bear.

Our trust in God on currency
does not wane in bad weather.

I keep things separate that come
In succession every 90 days or so.

The spring uses its own calendar
And has a valid reason for every late show.

I toss this penny in my wishing well.
There is a history of seasons in the copper of this coin.

The addendum to perfection

Compliant

How transient for the sun
To stay shorter than a lover

Not even until dawn-
To make me feel whorish

For basking in raw light-
Scandalous.

The addendum to perfection

Cooking

I like to scoop you up like a spatula
Flipping hotcakes off the girdle
-onto a bed of strawberries
-onto a swirl of whip cream
-into a mouthful of hungry love.

The addendum to perfection

Ravages of war

When I had something left to fight with, I truly believed that winning
The war was attainable.

I could come up with a strategy for combat situations with little rations,
Or sleep to rest me alert, during the day, fighting all through the advanced

Night falls glowing with conflict. Now that every turn is not trusted to curve
Into some safety and children are not only children when they explode for a
cause

Underneath a land mind, hidden too well too unearth, the Earth trembles
And the violence reaches every street.

The addendum to perfection

Ecosystem

Children spill milk in their cereal
Because of the weight of the cow

And the tree that became a carton
That can keep the sun out and recycle

Forests that want to live again and again with words
Etched in their bark between the lines

Of loose leaf notebooks or die when the milk sours
And the cereal becomes stale and the tree

Is discarded like a seed that grows into death
To sprout another life.

The addendum to perfection

Rush hour

Something was dead inside the body of a skunk
On the side of the road.

No one stopped to mourn in traffic
heavier than most funeral processions.

No minister robed in black with a thin white collar
To offset, spoke a kind word.

No organ piped even a dirge hard on the nostril
Opening in both ears.
Only the lack of appreciation for the food chain
And some road rage to justify a speeding ticket.

Nothing smells with such distinction
For the glory of recognition.

The addendum to perfection

24/7

We are always together holding even the second hand
Of the clock still, so that we will never be apart,

Separated in the space we occupy in each others arms
And that space which has been reserved for us before

We ever met, never knew time as a relationship without us-
Giving definition to words that take up time and even more space-

And space is best when it disappears between us the way air hides
Away from sight and we become the distance every couple measures

For the standard of what they treasure in the time they spend together
As the second hand overlaps the hour and for a moment the difference

Between them is lost in their similarity and we know that what we have
Will last after time is no more and space unoccupied leaves emptiness alone.

The addendum to perfection

For love

I sell all that I have for almost nothing
And I exist as an ad in the classified.

My body which I gave to be burned
For the highest sum, I wanted to save

For you and the promise of a barbecue-
Of a memorable picnic in the park.

For your affections I even severed limbs.
Who needs two hands and more than one foot anyway?

Maimed and down to bare essentials
I make love to you one expensive thought at a time.

The addendum to perfection

Sugar

I prefer you sweet-
Cubed with whitewalls on all six sides.

I'd roll you like dice against pavement
Recently wet from my touch.

Grab you with only the silver reflection
Of my stainless tongs.

Take your feet for a walk on vertical air.
Drink my tea with two lumps of you in my throat.

One right after the other fresh from the cane unrefined.

The addendum to perfection

Recollection

Remember the first time the weight of our bodies
Pressed the green lawn flat, one thousand blades of grass at a time?

The way we disappeared
One frame after another shutter speed not withstanding?

Remember all the dandelions competing for romantic
Divisions of real estate?

So many suns warm against our bodies revolving around
Each of us counter clockwise.

Soaking in rays of euphoria
Even after we were gone, remember.

The addendum to perfection

My beloved Valentine

You came to me burning in the passion of an incense stick:
When I rose from my knees, from my prayers bending

The very ears of God.
When the phone rang.

When the introduction fell
From the sky like rain, like small

Grains of white rice, to feed the birds.
Birds who clap like thunder in a crowd

When we exit the church and they fly
All at once, altogether to applaud, the newly weds.

The addendum to perfection

Passions

Sometimes we give our bodies to be burned
Or we burn before we give our bodies to each other,

And we know its better to marry ourselves with a vow
That will last through anniversaries, golden like the band

We both share, in their different respective sizes
as we measure up to our expectations with the rhythm

That we use to make our own music, with the voice we share
When we sing lyrics, in our own originality, in our own creative juice,

Heating things up to the boiling point, to the Fahrenheit, where love
Is steam rising from the union of our passion and we burn.

The addendum to perfection

Something touched me

Wet where I only understood dry
And sticky makes my mouth breathe underwater.

Open or closed, puckered up like a bubble of air,
Too big to be an apple in my throat rising over horizons

Or your tongue boring a whole into its core
Like a seed that loves to measure and circle

Circumference, something touched me raw.

The addendum to perfection

Adultery

The danger
Meeting early

when you are not free
To love with the liberty

That comes with status.
You hold back feelings

That find there way
Without your permission.

How do you refrain
From the reprise

That appears when you summon me
In every dream?

The addendum to perfection

A Biblical love

This is where I stop
And wait forging hope

Until you show.
I believe God

Will bring you
Even as He brought Rachel

To Jacob after seven years
And then another seven years.

I see past every Leah in my life
And every uncle is a Laban.

The addendum to perfection

After conversation

Think about how much we meant to each other
In the economy of words we used early in our chance meeting.

Meeting expectations we did not know we had or had to express
And when it happen it was an expression all by itself, without

The structure of definitions getting in the way of everything
that mattered most: coupled together in the shape of a pear,

Halved like a heart full of seeds, we ate the fruit
that might have been forbidden to the taste: but

In our mouths resting on the outer layer of skin that covers our lips
Like a stolen kiss leaving not even a print; we catch the smile

That is an intimate delicacy between us after conversation.

The addendum to perfection

Jewelry

The cross clings to Christ
Around the neck with gold

In carats enough for a king
No relic can capture the separation

Of God and Man, the division
Of the union when sin divides,

Or when truth restores at the crossroads
Of faith and disbelief.

The addendum to perfection

Why

When we were together
It was the best of times-

Apart it was the worst:
For what is life without breathing

The scent of your perfume?
Without knowing, what only

Lovers know, without intuition
To guide them to each other.

Without the faith to try to find
The single person that fits

Squarely with no missing or left over parts.
I want to know, why?

The addendum to perfection

Drought

So friendly clouds call sky
Its nickname," blue."

Birds chime in, stopping to consider
the captivity of flight.

Is fog still fog so far above ground?
Sheep do not huddle long

Where nothing grows vegetable green,
Without the taste of sod, without a finger

In the dirt, wet on the tip, every thirsty time
A seed wants a drink. Where are the clouds right now?

The addendum to perfection

October

Never wanted to be summer
Leaving foliage for some November.

And who would give up the harvest
For more rain if April, took its place?

No, the rake is already poised for the lawn
To clean like finger nails scratching dead skin

From the callous ground that has become
The surface on the bottom of your feet.

Put away the lemonade stand, upright, in the garage
Underneath, the wooden ladder, leaning like the tree

Dropping leaves in celebration
Of October.

The addendum to perfection

X

Reminders come with unwanted droppings from the mice
Who cohabitate underneath my roof.

The compromise of trust upon every counter top
Will only be restored with hard work of faith in sanitation.

Some things are only sterile after they have been disposed of
Others only grotesque in view of the truth that comes with hind sight.

Expenses mount with lessons that do not come free of charge.
Ignorance is the biggest expenditure I always forget to budget.

Now the only thing rabid in my life is the past.

The addendum to perfection

Sighting

Allow the moon to lactate
And everything white becomes milk all over again.

Darkness smears the night sky like the wet paint
A black cat brushed against some evening stars.

Daylight on the verge of ocean blue eyes motionless
Arrives.

The addendum to perfection

Two goals

I want to be the best poet produced in this century.
Second goal, defy the neurotic critic. Rouse their columns

Into a slumber, a veiled submission. I was born during the McCarthy Era
Some of the best poetry was birthed under bipartisan political fear.

My pen is not afraid of war mongers, of child slayers, of deal makers
And lies that deceive the liar. I can crumble paper the same way

Leaders are deposed, land them in a round metal waste basket
With bars like a prison, like an exilic looking for real estate.

The addendum to perfection

Maybe not, Haiku

I thought about it

But someone might

Mistake my daughter's name

For the poetry of Basho:

For a sunset that someone

Else saw on some horizon

That never laid down in front of me.

For thirteen characters

That might not be enough

To say everything

Inside an art form.

Inside a tiny life

Too big for short forms of poetry.

Too Japanese

For an African American girl.

The addendum to perfection

Such captions in the sky, daily

I can read clouds in any region
Without the science of interpretation.

The sun is harder to face, eye to eye.
Rain sends gifts before its arrival.

Snows hides in fear of definitions.
The wind embraces everything it surrounds

But never admits, the liability of directions.
I gaze at stars that shoot other stars

Wishing on the ones that fall, close to me.

The addendum to perfection

In the laundry room

You call out my name
During every spin cycle.

Some things are so deeply embedded
They may never come out.

I fold you with care
before I stack you on clean sheets.

No bleach can rinse
These thoughts in my head.

The addendum to perfection

Skinning dipping

The face of the moon quarters four times
Until it fills the circle of my expectation.

Evening stars dip in shallow waters, when no one is around
To view.

However, forest reach toward the sky in the reflection of the lake
Every wave still moves clouds in front of the sun up stream.

I only wade in currents that propel
Every stroke swims closer to you.

The addendum to perfection

Hiding in tall grass

Trees overlook camouflage for years
Never relocate in an open field.

So many stationary resentments
Take deep roots straight to China.

Yucca spears color as a conquest for Native Island people.
Paradise stays without the tourist attractions.

The sun stands taller than the forest purely for the aesthetic.
Careful eclectic reader, sheltering this much truth before a tree

Ever becomes a book is perplexing.

The addendum to perfection

Perfection

How lovely, settled in your disposition
Personally one on one, with a romantic letter,

With a flower that defies any great name.
Rare considering everyone and everything

That fits into my frame of reference.
I find the artist in all that is you and yours to create

In the medium of the shared life.
Stenciled along the borders of the heart with perfected trim

The décor finds a woman's touch.

The addendum to perfection

The addendum to perfection

True a touch is more than contact
On the surface of the skin, skin

That covers lips, lips thick and red
As wax candy, made for kissing

Made for eating, made for melting
in the searing heat of your touch.

The addendum to perfection

Amen

The strength of the sun at noon
Makes my longing for you a zenith,

Centered high East, middle sky blue.
So many wish for such a lover.

You not to be confused with starry first heavens
Or angels ascending as winged wonders, smile.

The addendum to perfection